Backyard Flowers

Flowers that bloom in spring

CROCUS

DAFFODIL

TULIP

Flowers that bloom in summer

IRIS

SNAPDRAGON

ROSE

Flowers that bloom in autumn

CHRYSANTHEMUM

ASTER

DAHLIA

Flowers that grow close to the ground

PANSY

ENGLISH DAISY

FORGET-ME-NOT

Flowers that grow 5 to 12 inches above the ground

PETUNIA

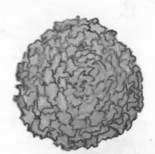

MARIGOLD

ZINNIA

Flowers that grow tall

SUNFLOWER

GLADIOLUS

HOLLYHOCK

BEGINNING
KNOWLEDGE
BOOKS

Beginning Knowledge Books are for the young reader who is eager to learn about the world around him. Beautiful color illustrations and simple words are guides that offer a wealth of carefully chosen answers for young questioners. The editors of the Beginning Knowledge Books are grateful for the expert assistance of: Miss Amy Clampitt, Librarian, National Audubon Society, 1952-59, in checking the text; Mr. Robert Christatos, in checking the illustrations.

The Beginning Knowledge Book of
Backyard Flowers

by Polly Hathaway/Illustrated by Raul Mina Mora

CONTENTS

TULIP	ROSE	GLADIOLUS
CROCUS	IRIS	SNAPDRAGON
DAFFODIL	PEONY	MARIGOLD
HYACINTH	PANSY	SUNFLOWER
VIOLET	PETUNIA	ZINNIA
ENGLISH DAISY	CORNFLOWER	CHRYSANTHEMUM

A RUTLEDGE BOOK

Copyright © 1965, by Rutledge Books, Inc.
Prepared and produced for The Macmillan Company, New York
Collier-Macmillan Limited, London
Collier-Macmillan Canada, Ltd., Toronto, Ontario
All rights reserved. Library of Congress catalog card number: 65-20624
Printed in U.S.A.
Third Printing 1967

Backyard Flowers

Flowers add beauty to the world around us.

Their scent makes the air sweet. They also have

many uses. Bees, moths, and other insects feed on

their nectar. So do some birds. Many flowers

are used in cooking, in perfumes, and in

medicines.

Flowers grow almost everywhere. The water

lily grows in lakes. The prickly-pear

cactus blooms in the dry desert. The Christmas

rose grows up through the snow.

We could not live without flowers, for without

them we would have no vegetables, no grain

to make bread, and no fruits.

Most plants grow from seeds. To learn how seeds are made, look at an Easter lily.

In the center of the flower stands a straight, thin spike. This is called the pistil. The rounded lower part of the pistil is the ovary.

Inside the ovary are tiny ovules. These will become the seeds. All around the pistil are shorter, thinner spikes. These are called stamens. At the tips of the stamens are anthers. The anthers hold many tiny specks of dust called pollen.

Pollen must reach an ovule in order to form a new seed. This is usually done with the help of insects, which carry the pollen from one flower to another. Once the ovule has received pollen, the seeds begin to form.

Properly planted in garden dirt, a flower seed sends out a ___ shoot that grows up through the ground. From within the shoot grows a bud that will blossom into a flower.

Although all flowers come from seeds to begin with, some are grown in gardens from underground buds called bulbs. Inside each bulb are all the parts of the new plant. Some bulbs can remain in the ground year after year. The daffodil is one of these. Other bulbs must be dug up each fall and kept in a cool, dry place. Two other types of underground bud are the corm and the rhizome. The gladiolus develops from a corm; the iris develops from a rhizome.

Other flowers are grown from underground

stems known as tubers.   One flower that

grows from a tuber is the dahlia.   Some flowers

are grown from cuttings—a small part of the plant

cut off and put into water or soil to develop roots.

Geraniums   are usually grown from cuttings.

Many flowering plants die after they bloom, and

new seeds must be planted the next spring. These

are called annuals. The marigold is one annual.

Some flowers, like crocuses,   come

up and bloom year after year. These are called

perennials. Other flowers are planted one year to

bloom the next. The pansy   is such a flower.

Taking care of a flower garden is fun.

At the end of this book is a plan to help you

grow a garden of your own.

Tulip

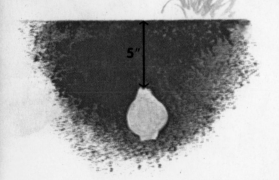

Tulips are grown from bulbs. To have tulips blooming in the spring, the bulbs must be put into the ground late in fall.

5"

Tulips come in many colors. Some combine two colors, so that the blossoms are brightly striped, and others have petals with ruffled edges of a second color. If you look closely at a tulip, you will see the pistil and stamens.

In gardens, tulips are usually grown from bulbs planted in the fall for blooming the next spring. The bulbs should be put into the ground late in the fall. If planted too early they will start to grow and may be killed by frost.

Like most plants that grow from bulbs, tulips are perennials. Bulbs are like underground storehouses. After one year's flowers bloom and die, a bud made up of tiny new stems, leaves, and flowers forms in the bulb in the ground. It does not start to grow until the warmth of spring.

Tulip blossoms come in many colors—
bright red, yellow, gold. Some
combine colors, so that the top and
bottom of the flower are different.

Crocus

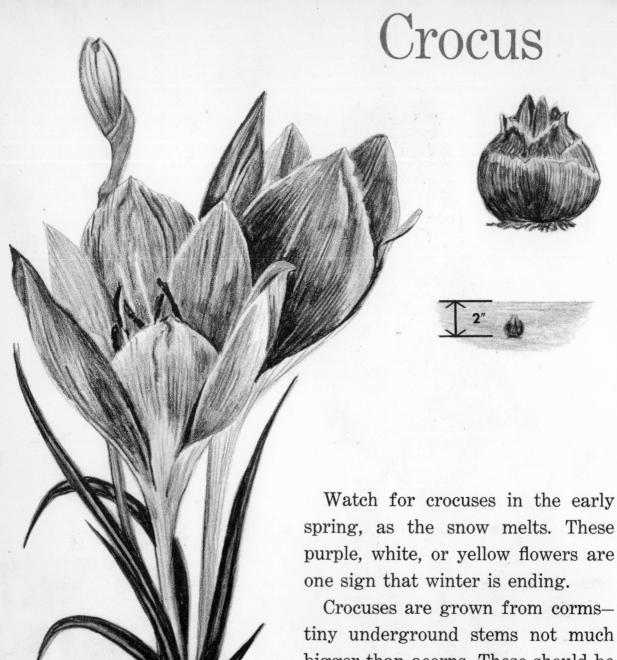

2"

Crocuses are grown from corms—
tiny acorn-like stems. These
should be planted in early fall.

Watch for crocuses in the early spring, as the snow melts. These purple, white, or yellow flowers are one sign that winter is ending.

Crocuses are grown from corms—tiny underground stems not much bigger than acorns. These should be planted in the fall, before the first frost, from 3 to 4 inches under the ground. Gardeners often plant them in large beds to make a bright splash of color in the early spring before anything else is in bloom.

Daffodil

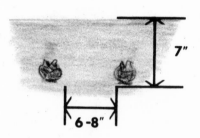

7"

6-8"

Daffodils bloom in early spring, soon after the crocuses. They are most often yellow or white, but in some daffodils the trumpet at the center of the flower is deep orange or red-orange.

Daffodils grow from bulbs, which come in several sizes. The bigger the bulb, the deeper it should go into the ground. The bulbs need 6 or 7 inches of soil to cover them. All daffodil bulbs should be planted early in the fall before the first frost.

Like tulips, daffodils are grown from bulbs. They should be planted in early fall.

Hyacinth

A member of the lily family, hyacinths grow in a cluster of fragrant blossoms around a straight, thick stalk. They are various shades of pink or blue, as well as white.

Hyacinth bulbs should be planted in the fall, about 6 inches deep. They are hardy plants and do well in most gardens as long as the ground is not too damp. If it is, the bulbs will rot and there will be no hyacinths in your garden.

Hyacinths can also be grown indoors. Plant them in small pots and set the pots in a cool, dark place—a cellar or closet—until the shoots are about 3 inches high and the flower buds are beginning to show. Then bring them into a light place, but not in direct sunlight, for two days. Finally, move them to a spot where they will get the sunshine.

Hyacinth bulbs should be planted 6 inches underground. They should not be watered too often and need lots of sunshine.

The curled petals of the hyacinth
are a familiar sight in many gardens.
These fragrant blossoms grow in a
cluster around a straight stalk.

Violet

Violets are found in many gardens of the world and can be white, yellow, or purple.

Violets are a favorite flower in many parts of the world. They grow easily—in fact, they will take up too much of a garden if they are not thinned out.

The flowers of the violet are usually half hidden behind the big, heart-shaped leaves. There are white and yellow violets, but the purple ones are more common.

Violets will grow from seeds or cuttings, and can be planted in either the spring or fall.

English Daisy

The flowers of the English daisy may be white, pink, or deep rose. They bloom in the spring, but must be planted in July or August the year before. They do well in any soil, and are often planted with pansies or forget-me-nots.

English daisies may wilt during the first hot days, but if the wilted flowers are picked off, the plants will continue to bloom. They often re-seed themselves and come up to bloom a second year.

The English daisy blooms in the spring. Its flowers can be pink, white, or deep rose.

Rose

Roses come in many different colors, from white and yellow to pink and red. Rose stems are covered with sharp thorns.

There are many different kinds of roses—roses that climb, and some that grow quite close to the ground. And there are many different colors, from white and yellow to many shades of pink and red.

Many kinds of roses grow wild. From these wild roses, gardeners and florists have developed all the hundreds of varieties of roses that we know today.

Roses need a lot of water, and are easy to grow in most soils, but they cannot live in soggy ground. For garden roses, a well-drained, sunny place is best, although they will grow in light shade. Most garden roses grow from small plants put into the ground in early spring.

When you pick roses, it's best to cut them with scissors, for their stems have many sharp thorns.

Put small rose plants in the ground in early spring before the buds begin to show. Roses grow best in well-drained soil, in a sunny spot.

Iris

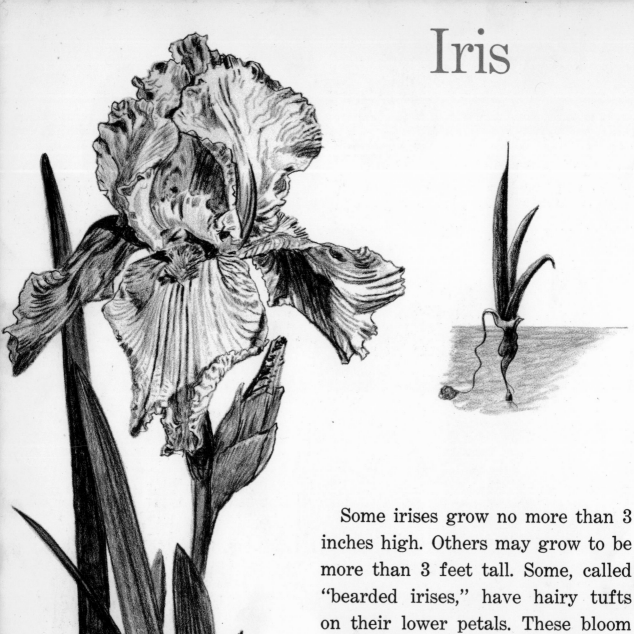

Irises grow from fleshy roots called rhizomes. Plant them no deeper than 1 inch underground.

Some irises grow no more than 3 inches high. Others may grow to be more than 3 feet tall. Some, called "bearded irises," have hairy tufts on their lower petals. These bloom later than the others.

Most irises grow from fleshy roots called rhizomes. These should be planted no deeper than about 1 inch underground. Rhizomes multiply in the soil. Every few years they must be dug up, divided into sections, and each section re-planted separately.

Peony

Peony plants, once they have begun to grow well, will bloom for many years. The flowers are white, pink, or deep red. If you cut them before they are in full bloom, they will last many days in water.

Peonies grow from tubers—thick, knob-like pieces of stem on which there are small buds, like the "eyes" of a potato. Plant the tubers in the fall, with the eyes 2 inches below the surface. If planted too deep, they may bud but not bloom.

Peonies grow from thick pieces of stem called tubers. Plant tubers in fall 2 inches underground.

Pansy

The pansy has been a favorite garden flower for many generations. Because of the spots of color—generally yellows, purples, and brownish tones—on the petals, the flower looks like a face.

Seeds for pansies should be put into the ground in early spring for late-summer bloom, or in August for flowering the following spring.

Once pansies have begun to bloom, a little care will keep them in flower for several months. Pick them before the blossom begins to wilt. New flowers will blossom quickly.

If the plants become spindly, cut them off about 1½ inches above the ground. With your hands or a tool, work fertilizer into the soil around the pansies. In a short time, the plants will grow back and begin to flower again.

Pansies grow from seeds and can be planted either in the early spring or in August. Pansies will stay in flower all the summer months.

The yellow, brown, and purple spots
of color on the petals of pansies give
these flowers the look of a face.
The pansy is an easy flower to grow.

Petunia

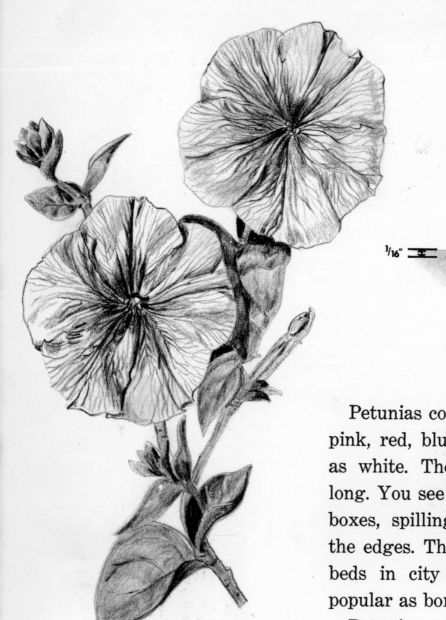

1/16"

Petunias are grown from seeds and should be planted in the spring. Cut the petunias that grow too tall.

Petunias come in lovely shades of pink, red, blue, and purple, as well as white. They bloom all summer long. You see them often in window boxes, spilling their blossoms over the edges. They make pretty flower beds in city parks, and they are popular as border plants in gardens.

Petunias are grown from seeds planted in the spring. If the plants grow too tall, cut them back. They will soon grow into bushy plants again. Pick the petunias often.

Cornflower

Cornflowers will grow well even in poor, sandy soil. The seeds should be planted in the fall for flowers early in the spring. When the ground warms up, plant more seeds. If you plant some every two weeks after that, you will have cornflowers in bloom all summer long. It is a hardy flower and can re-seed itself.

There are pink and white cornflowers, but more often they are a deep, clear blue. They are also called bachelor's buttons.

Cornflower seeds should be planted early in spring, when the ground warms up. These are hardy flowers.

Gladiolus

The gladiolus grows from a corm. Corms should be planted when the sun warms the ground and dug up in the fall to be stored.

The gladiolus needs little care and will give flowers for cutting all summer long. It comes in many colors and shades, from white and palest pink through reds, oranges, yellows, and lavenders to deepest purple. Few flowers grow so well in so many different climates. It grows best in well-drained soil.

The gladiolus is grown from a corm, which is a fleshy stem shaped like a flat bulb. The gladiolus corm cannot live underground through the cold winter months. The corms must be dug up in the fall and stored until spring.

The corms should be planted as soon as the sun warms the ground. After the flowers bloom, the corm withers and a new one grows on top of it. The new corm is the one that should be dug up and stored.

The blossoms of the gladiolus come
in many colors, from white and pink
to red, orange, yellow, and purple.
The gladiolus grows tall and straight.

Snapdragon

Snapdragons grow from seeds and should be planted in the spring just below the top of the ground.

Snapdragons may be white, yellow, orange, or any of the shades from pink to deepest red. They grow to different heights, but the most common garden varieties are about 18 inches tall. Gardeners often plant snapdragons as a border against a fence or along a wall.

In mild climates snapdragons are perennials—they come up every year. But if you live where the winters are cold, new snapdragon seeds must be planted each spring.

Marigold

Marigolds bloom from midsummer until the first frost. Their colors are those of fall leaves—yellow, gold, orange, tawny red—and they have a strong, tangy scent.

There are dwarf marigolds which are only a few inches high, and there are other varieties that grow as tall as 4 feet. All marigolds are easy to grow. The seeds can be planted in the garden in early spring in almost any kind of soil. The plants do well in sun, but will grow in shade as well.

Marigold seeds are planted in early spring. The blossoms of the marigold have a tangy smell.

Sunflower

Even though sunflowers are rooted to one spot, they are not without movement. They do something which few other flowers do—they turn their heads toward the sun. If you watch closely, you can see the sunflower blossoms turn to follow the sun across the sky.

Sunflowers grow wild in parts of the Middle West. Both the wild and the garden sunflowers are grown from seeds and flourish in the hottest sun. Some sunflowers grow to be 15 feet tall. The blossom can grow to 12 inches in diameter.

Some people eat sunflower seeds. And they are often fed to birds. The oil made from the seeds is used in making soap and paint. In parts of Europe, the leaves of sunflowers are fed to cattle, and the stems are burned for fuel.

Sunflowers are grown from seeds and do well in hot sun. Sunflower seeds are eaten by birds, and the leaves are fed to cattle.

If you are patient and watch closely, you will see the sunflower turn to follow the sun across the sky. The sunflower can grow to be 15 feet tall.

Zinnia

Plant zinnia seeds in spring with plenty of space between. Zinnias do well in most soils.

Zinnias are among the easiest flowers to grow, for they do well in almost any soil. They flourish in bright sun, but do almost as well in a little shade.

There are tiny zinnias and big branching ones that grow 3 feet tall. Zinnias bloom all summer. The more you pick them, the more they will bloom. Do not plant zinnia seeds until all danger of frost is past. The plants need room to spread, so leave plenty of space between them.

Chrysanthemum

Chrysanthemums have been grown in the gardens of China for thousands of years. These colorful flowers bloom in the fall, when summer's last blossoms are fading.

Many people plant chrysanthemums in the fall, but this is a mistake. Although they will bloom until the first frost, they may not live through the winter. Put plants in the ground in spring. Chrysanthemums should be planted where there is plenty of sun. They do best in well-drained soil.

Chrysanthemums should be planted in the spring where there is a lot of sun. They bloom in the fall.

Garden Plan

Here is a garden that is planned so that there will be flowers in bloom from the early spring through late autumn.

Start in the fall. In a sunny spot, dig the soil until it is fine. Plant daffodil bulbs first, tulips later. Daffodils—shorter and first to bloom—should be in front. Dig 5 to 7 inches deep. Put bonemeal in each hole. Bonemeal is fertilizer. Put in the bulbs—flat side down—and cover them with dirt.

On a warm spring day, plant the zinnias and marigolds. Follow the directions on the seed packages.

Put out chrysanthemum plants in May. Put bonemeal and some water into each hole. As the branches start to grow, pinch off their tips to keep the plants bushy. Water and weed regularly and you will have a beautiful garden.

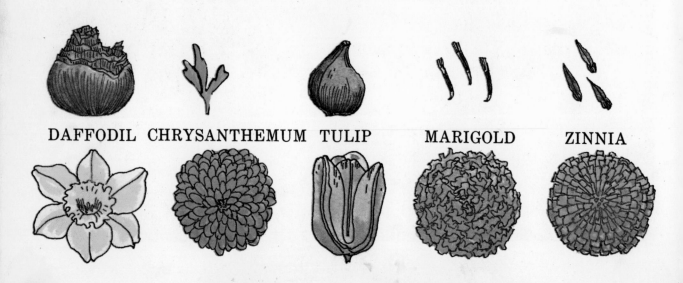

DAFFODIL   CHRYSANTHEMUM   TULIP   MARIGOLD   ZINNIA

GARDEN PLAN

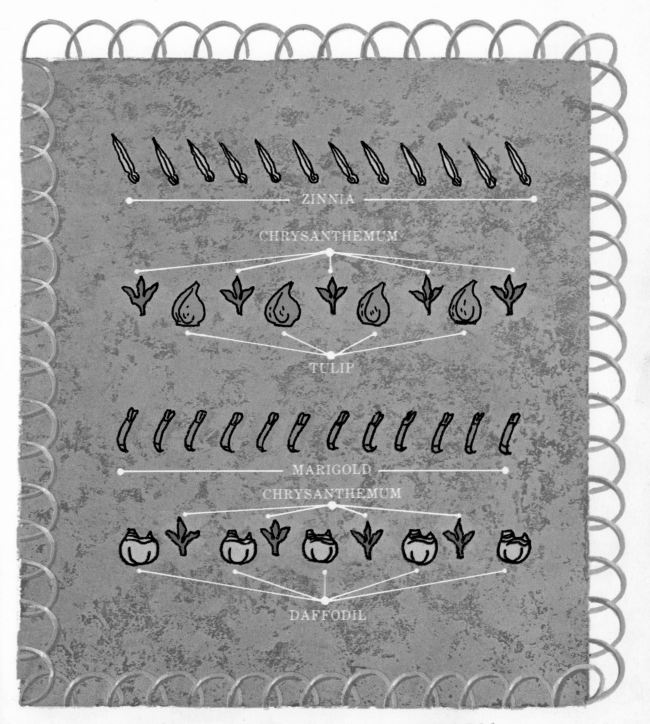